How to Deal with Bullies

A Guide to Stop Bullying and Help Your Child Recover from the Effects of Bullying

by Kathleen Bishopson

Table of Contents

Introduction...1

Chapter 1: Understanding the Bullying Phenomenon.
....5

Chapter 2: Kinds of Bullying...11

Chapter 3: Signs of Bullying..15

Chapter 4: Identifying a Bully.......................................19

Chapter 5: Preventing Your Child from Being a
Victim of Bullying..23

Chapter 6: Protecting Your Bullied Child..................33

Chapter 7: Recovering from Bullying...........................41

Conclusion..47

Introduction

Parents react differently when their child is bullied – some are frightened, others are enraged, while a few pretend that it doesn't matter to them. The truth: bullying is a big deal and it should be dealt with effective force at the soonest possible time. If left unchecked, bullied children suffer both physically and psychologically, and the abuse might even haunt them well into their adult years. DO NOT LET THIS HAPPEN TO YOUR FAMILY. Do the right thing and arm yourself with valuable anti-bullying knowledge for your children and their future children's sakes.

This book contains proven steps and strategies on how to prevent bullying, protect your child, and help them recover and rebuild their self-esteem after the trauma of being bullied.

Thanks again for purchasing this book. I hope you enjoy it!

Chapter 1: Understanding the Bullying Phenomenon

If you found out that your child is the target of bullying, you might have the following reactions:

1. You shrug it off, saying to yourself that it's not a big deal and kids bully and get bullied all the time.

2. You boil with rage and you dream up ways of punishing your child's tormentor.

3. You demand your child to take revenge against the bully because it builds character.

4. You blame the teachers and school personnel for not giving proper attention to the students.

5. You get flooded by intense emotions stemming from your own childhood experiences of being bullied.

6. You become paralyzed because you're overwhelmed by the situation and you're unsure of what to do next.

Whatever your initial reactions may be, it's important for you to acknowledge that bullying is serious and your child is in real need of help. Bullying is not child's play – it is abuse and it should be treated as such. To react rashly or do nothing at all is unwise, and it usually worsens the situation. Let's take a look at each scenario.

1. Apathy. The worst thing you can do is to ignore what's happening. Being bullied is stressful to a child, and it's likely that one doesn't receive support from school or peers. As your children's primary caretaker, it's your responsibility to make them feel that somebody cares. It's your duty to help improve their circumstances to give them a better shot at life.

2. Retaliation. Revenge may feel good, but it seldom solves problems and escalates them instead. It also teaches your child to be the bully himself, and this should worry you because bullies are likely to become criminals when they grow up. Do not fight fire by fire, but seek intelligent actions to stop the bullying in its tracks.

3. Leaving the child alone. Bullying involves a strong person of whatever age dominating a

weak target. Don't set unrealistic expectations for your kids; it will increase their stress levels and make them more vulnerable to the attacks. Instead, seek the cooperation of those who can affect the bully's behavior effectively.

4. Placing the blame on others. Teachers are not omniscient and omnipresent and they can't know what's going on with your child every minute of the day. Blaming them may only strain your relationship, and may make them less receptive to your needs. Talk with them civilly and work together to find ways to solve bullying in their classrooms.

5. Being emotional. Don't let yourself be engulfed by your past but focus on your child's present. You need clarity of mind to handle this challenging situation; do your best to calm down your feelings and see the bigger picture.

6. Being paralyzed. Arm yourself with useful information about bullying. Make a simple plan on what to do and tackle the issue one step at a time. Remember: you have to do something because not doing anything will make it harder for both of you. Bullying

should never be tolerated for the sake of your children and their future.

It's normal to have any or even many of these reactions; but it doesn't mean that you have to continue with your initial instinctual response. Reading this book is a good move for both you and your young one, since ample knowledge guides you to do the right things and avoid bad choices.

Bullying Defined

Bullying is not good-natured fun; it is a harmful and abusive act that is repeated frequently to a victim. These victims may be chosen at random or targeted because of a trait. Bullies often choose targets that are:

- Physically weaker than they are

- Different than most of their peers (in appearance, stature, etc.)

- Have strange hobbies or mannerisms

- Submissive

- Reactive (easily provoked)

- Have bad hygiene

- Have few or no friends

- Have poor social skills
- Have difficulty expressing themselves

- Have low grades

- Have low self esteem

- Even handicapped physically or mentally

In short, the victim is seen as inferior to the bully, has little social support, and does not have the capability of fighting back. To protect your child from being bullied, you have to do your best so that your child will not seem like easy prey. You will read more about these protective measures in Chapter 5.

Chapter 2: Kinds of Bullying

There's a misconception that bullying only involves physical assaults. This is a dangerous notion because it implies that people can ignore psychological bullying. Emotional trauma is as valid as tangible wounds and injuries, and if left untreated, the pain may persist for a child's entire life.

- Physical. It's easy to notice whether a child is physically abused – you see bruises, scars, and sometimes even broken bones. Some examples of brute force bullying are private space invasion, punching, kicking, tripping, scratching, slapping, hair pulling, shoving, and giving wedgies. When things get out of hand, weapons may be used and cause serious damage.

- Emotional. Physical attacks also affect a young person's emotions, but there are bullying methods that are purely psychological. It has been observed that girls are more likely to do emotional bullying. Examples are public humiliation, excluding someone from a group, verbal taunting, spreading gossip, manipulation with the use of threats, telling a lie about a child to put them in trouble, and causing them to feel bad about themselves in other ways. Although the emotional kind of bullying may seem tame compared to physical scuffles, it may be potent enough to cause a child to contemplate suicide.

Children's well-being rests not only with their physical health but also in their emotional state. Pay attention to both so you develop an awareness of their capabilities of coping with the presence of a bully in their life. The next chapters will give you plenty of ideas on how to do this.

Chapter 3: Signs of Bullying

Bullying has a powerful effect on people and, unless your child is good at hiding his or her troubles or you don't pay much attention, it will leave noticeable marks on your child. Look out for these telltale signs:

- Bruises, wounds, and other injuries

- Messed up appearance

- Soiled clothes and belongings

- Damaged or missing possessions

- Change in sleeping patterns – insomnia, oversleeping, frequent nightmares, etc.

- Pretending to be sick

- Bedwetting (especially if he has never done it before or he's over 7 years old)

- Crying for no apparent reason

- Aloof demeanor

- Sudden outbursts of emotion

- Irritability

- Uncharacteristic behavior

- Failing grades

- Sudden lack of interest in hobbies

- Reluctance to attend school or visit other places he used to frequent

- Depression

Chapter 4: Identifying a Bully

Why Bullying Happens

Bullying is a widespread phenomena and it has been going on throughout history. It occurs because most people, even young kids, have a natural tendency for being aggressive towards others. Some are born with a tendency to become bullies, while others are raised in an environment that encouraged bullying behavior.

Bullies have these characteristics:

- Have higher levels of aggression

- Appear to have confidence in themselves

- Crave attention

- Enjoy emotional reactions towards them

- Delight in being dominant

- Know how to exert influence

- Are unable to put themselves in their victims' shoes

- Do not feel remorse about what they do

- May be struggling with something and reacting with aggressive behavior

People learn from what they see. When their parents are abusive, there's a chance that they will be abusive, too. In fact, according to one study, a great majority of child bullies have parents that are bullies too. It's also likely that the media and computer games contribute to bullying behavior because they popularize aggression and violence among impressionable minds. No matter what may have caused bullies to become the way they are, you should let them know that what they do is unacceptable and prevent them from harming your children.

Chapter 5: Preventing Your Child from Being a Victim of Bullying

Being at the receiving end of a bully's whims is no picnic for children. Although it's possible to recover from being bullied, it's best if you prevent your child from being targeted in the first place. Once started, a bullying episode will continue on and on unless active interventions are made. If the bully is still in target-searching mode, make your son or daughter uninteresting to him by doing the following:

- Withholding attention from the bully

- Seeking help from peers

- Calling the attention of authorities

- Being assertive

- Having high self-esteem

- Having friends

- Belonging to the crowd

Withholding Attention

Teach your child to withhold what the bully is seeking. A bully wants victims who make him feel powerful. He does this by making them feel enraged, frightened, annoyed, uncomfortable, etc. The more the bully gets to control their emotions, the happier he gets. If someone is provoking your child, train him to ignore the provoker. That will make him boring for the bully and he'll seek a more entertaining participant.

Ignoring the bully may be hard especially for a normally reactive child. A method for keeping calm despite provocation is to count from one to ten while taking deep breaths. Teach your kids to walk away and avoid the bully for as much as they can. Let them know that bullies are thrilled when they get people to react in any way; if they don't show emotions, the bullies get nothing and will eventually move on.

Seeking Help from Peers

There are more non-bullies than bullies. Encourage your child to form groups with other people who are against bullying. An outnumbered bully quickly loses motivation. Talk with your child's playmates and classmates (and their parents) and tell them that if they band together and protect one another, they will be able to defeat a domineering bully.

Calling the Attention of Authorities

Reporting a bully may be scary for children, but it's usually very effective. Telling a teacher or the school principal about the bully's misdeeds increases the chances that the bully will be dealt with by appropriate punishment. The reports and the consequences should be consistent to teach the errant child that bullying will not be tolerated. You can request that these authorities do not divulge who reported the bully to protect him from the bully's ire.

Coordinate with people who can prevent bullying in the places where your child stays, may it be in the school, the playground, or a friend's house. Set guidelines about bullying and the consequences. Bullying becomes non-existent when a team of responsible adults are cooperating together to prevent bullies from acting out on their impulses.

Being Assertive

A bully loves a docile victim; when he encounters resistance, he will have second thoughts of continuing his attempts. Practice assertiveness with your young ones. Encourage them to speak their mind in a rational manner instead of lashing out or clamming up. Let them know that it's okay to acknowledge their feelings, and that they have the right to confront a bully assertively if he's disturbing him/her in some way.

A bully's strength depends on how he gets a victim to become emotionally wrecked and lose his or her wits. Defend your children against this tactic by making them keep their cool. While you're at home, practice how to react when a bully does certain things – this will decrease the pressure of thinking about what to do during the act of bullying. You can likewise use the bully's trick against himself by instructing your kids to make the bully think about what he's doing and forcing him to switch gears.

Emotional self-control is important in being assertive. Aggressiveness involves dominating another person through manipulation of the other's emotions. Passiveness is submitting to the bully's actions out of fear or indifference. Assertiveness is knowing what's right and sticking by it. Being assertive may be difficult for your kids at first, but the more that they practice it, the more effortless it becomes. The trick to developing assertiveness in your brood is to exhibit the trait yourself and to constantly give genuine and specific compliments whenever you observe them behave in an assertive manner.

Having High Self Esteem

When kids have high self-esteem, they will not bow down to a bully's antics and they will give a bully a harder time to feed on their insecurities. Enhance your young ones' view of themselves through the following techniques:

- Always be there for them. Kids consider themselves to be valuable when they know that somebody values them. Try your very best to be present especially when they need you the most. Listen to the things they tell you even though these topics might not be that interesting to you. Know about what's important to them, what they like and dislike, know their plans for the future and what happens to them daily. Spend quality time with them and help resolve their predicaments. Guide their actions lovingly, without resorting to humiliations and corporal punishments. Make them know you that you care. Just knowing that you love them may be enough to embed their worth in their mind and shield them from the bully's predatory nature.

- Compliment them: their grooming habits, their taste of clothes, their musical talents, their kindness to a schoolmate, their helpfulness when you're doing the chores, etc. Make sure that you mean it and it's something that is clear – saying "I really like the way you helped me with washing the dishes" has more impact than muttering vaguely, "You're a good girl." These genuine praises not only make children feel good, they also motivate them to do more of the same nice things.

- Help children deal with self-esteem issues. No child is perfect, and there's bound to be something that your child dislikes about himself or herself. Have a friendly conversation with your kiddos and ask what they're not comfortable with. It could be anything from looks, weight, skills, to the experiences they have at school. Formulate plans on how to solve their dilemmas if it's possible, if not, make them see these difficulties in a way that's easier to manage. For example, if a daughter is unhappy because she's overweight, you can find some age-appropriate exercises for her. If a son dislikes being the youngest in class, you can tell him that being the youngest means he's more advanced than his older classmates.

- Make your children develop positive beliefs. Children's beliefs greatly affect the way they handle what happens to them. Nurture supportive thoughts and correct weakening ones. Change distressing and inaccurate notions like "I'm a failure" into "I am having problems with Math right now, so I will set aside time to practice regularly until I become really good at it." Find mottos for them to recite whenever they feel challenged. Statements like "I can find solutions to my problems" or "I am always worthy and loved" bolster self-esteem in the face of ego-crushing trials.

- Let them do empowering things. For as long as it is safe for them, let them do what they like doing. It boosts children's confidence when they get to perform what they consider as worthwhile activity. You give them the impression that what they want matters, thus they matter too. The psychological rewards of participating and even excelling in a hobby translate into higher self-esteem, which is something that repels bullies.

Having Friends

If your children have friends, a bully will consider them as a tougher target because they will fear that their buddies will gang up on him afterwards. Aside from that, having companions around secures their self-worth and makes them confident enough to brush off a bully's intimidations.

To help your child make friends:

- Observe together how other children make friends and interact with each other.

- Guide your children in how to introduce themselves to a group of people.

- Teach them how to be polite and kind.

- Let them join other kids similar to them, like those who play their favorite sport, same-age groups, etc.

- Discuss about important matters about friendship, such as how to pick friends carefully, how to keep friendships, and how to resolve conflicts between friends.

Belonging to the Crowd

Bullies target those who are distinct; after all, being unique is easily equated to being weak because there's strength in numbers. It may go against the common admonition that kids should be encouraged to stand out, but practically, kids can avoid capturing the eye of a bully if they blend in the crowd. Know what's 'in' and what's 'out' among your child's peer group and give your children what they need so they can belong. However, see to it that they don't conform to behaviors and fads that are harmful to her. This is where your repository of wisdom for being older comes in handy.

Chapter 6: Protecting Your Bullied Child

Don't turn a blind eye when your child is currently a bullying victim. Consider the following consequences of being bullied:

- Continuation of the bullying behaviors

- Physical and psychological trauma

- Ill health

- Avoidance of school and other places where the bully might be

- Difficulty in forming and maintaining relationships

- Isolation

- Paranoia

- Anger

- Depression

- Helplessness

- Low self-esteem

- Poor academic performance

- Lost career opportunities

- Self-harm and possibility of suicide

As you can imagine, bullying needs intervention at the soonest possible time. Protect a bullied child by carrying out the appropriate suggestions in the previous chapters and accomplishing these additional things:

Know what's going on. When you notice these signs in a kid, ask straightforward questions: whether there are mean students in the school, what they do, and who they bully. You may also try asking friends or classmates to get a better view on what's happening within your child's social circles. Have a talk with your child's teachers and caretakers to find out if he or she is having any problems.

Let your children tell you what you need to hear. It may be difficult to listen to your kids' stories of being victims, but it will help tremendously if they have someone to air their grievances to. Let them speak uninterruptedly. Avoid butting in with your opinions and exclamations. Do not be emotional about their revelations to avoid contributing to their emotional burden. Aim to get all the facts so that you'll know what you're dealing with, who's involved, and what to do.

Getting Past Their Resistance to Talk

Bullied children may be reluctant to speak because of the following:

- Fear that the bully might get even. Convince your child that speaking up will help put a stop to the bullying. It has been observed that bullies escalate their actions when nobody resists or reports it. Assure bullied kids that you will do your very best so that they will not be harmed even if the bully gets reported and dealt with.

- Your children may think that you won't understand them. Refrain from making insults or having unrealistic expectations. Share your own childhood memories of being a bully's victim yourself. Listen without being judgmental. You may seek a guidance counselor or a psychologist to get professional help in this tricky situation.

- They may doubt that you can do anything to help. Make a commitment to protect your children from bullies. Do not run away from the problem; if you're uneasy about tackling the bullying singlehandedly, think about partnering with other parents or an anti-bullying group. Go to your children's parent-teacher conferences and bring up the topic. Ask your kids what they want you to do. Don't promise too much, but strive to do what you can.

- They're embarrassed to admit that they're being picked upon. Assure your children that being bullied is not something to be embarrassed about; in fact, it is the bully who should be ashamed. Boost their self-esteem (see Chapter 5) so that bullies will not succeed in weakening them psychologically.

- They believe that they deserve to be bullied. Talk about this belief. Let them specify what made them have that thought and what's keeping them from discarding the thought. Remind them of how valuable they are by pointing out their positive traits, past successes, and what's lovable about them. Explain that nobody deserves to be bullied for any reason, and that the bully has issues that need strict correction and not your child.

When your children open up to you, make them know that you appreciate their trust and honesty. Always talk to them so they'll feel comfortable in discussing things with you.

Help Your Children Avoid the Bully

Your children may spend most of their hours worrying about encountering a bully. To lessen their anxieties, help identify problematic areas that are conducive to bullying, such as places without guards, dim corners, tight spots, and so on. This skill will also be useful later on in adult life – criminals often hang out in secluded allies for example.

Report locations where bullies often hang out. Security features such as CCTV cameras, security guards, light installations, furniture modifications, and fences can greatly reduce bullying incidents. If it's allowed to do so and if this is something you are comfortable with, you can let your child bring a legal defensive weapon such as pepper spray to keep potential attackers at bay.

Caution your children to avoid places where there's no one around. Have them walk and stay in places where people can see and report bullying attacks. It's best to be at the presence of adults, but when it's not possible, they should at least hang out where their friends are.

Make It Difficult for the Bully to Continue Bullying

It's easy for bullies to feign innocence without evidence; document the bullying so you'll have something to show to the authorities. It will also come in handy when you decide to take matters to court. Get witnesses to testify against the bully. Gather the support of your child's peers and unite them into putting the bully in his proper place. Tell them that if the bully is ignored or resisted by many, he will no longer be a threat to anyone. Many children side with the bully out of fear of being chosen as a target; if everyone is against him, they won't have to pretend to be friends with the mean bully anymore.

Work with Everyone

Everyone should work hand in hand to fight bullying: the teachers, school officials, law enforcers, students, and everyone who is exposed to bullying. A bully is considered to be addicted to his bullying tendencies: as a power-hungry predator, he needs to be kept in check constantly and punished whenever he does something he shouldn't do. On the other hand, bullied victims should be empowered so that they will recuperate from the harm they have sustained from the abuses. Bystanders should be motivated to heed their conscience and avoid being swept away by the crowd or a compelling bully. Large-scale measures should be implemented to keep everyone safe from a bully's poor self-control and lack of empathy; it's for the bully and your children's ultimate good.

Chapter 7: Recovering from Bullying

Bullying can be traumatic for a child, especially one who is sensitive or has sustained repeated abuse. It's vital for the victim to heal from trauma because unresolved issues cause problems later on in life, as mentioned previously. As much as parents would want their children to get over it, recovery takes place gradually and may span years. The good thing is that bullied kids can live normal and satisfying lives despite the tribulations they have undergone.

- Join anti-bullying groups. There are many organizations that aim to protect bullied children, and these groups actively participate in anti-bullying endeavors. Find one near you – when you join such organizations, you will be more informed about how to combat bullying and you'd have a wide support system for your child. Your kids will also get to interact with other children and have opportunities to hone their social skills.

- Read more material about bullying and counteracting it. This book has provided you with the essentials of coping with bullying; if there are topics that interest you, feel free to explore more about them in other sources. You will find no end to material that will help your child overcome being bullied. Impart the knowledge you gain to your child to make him better equipped with understanding and coming to terms with bullies.

- Research about bullied individuals who coped and lived successful lives. As mentioned previously, people learn a lot from others. Celebrities like Oprah Winfrey, Rihanna, and Justin Timberlake are not exempted from being bullied at some point in their lives. Perhaps you have relatives or friends who you admire for their resiliency. Let your child know people who were bullied when they were young but came out the victors as they grew up. This will assure that your child can do the same. Investigate their strategies and who helped them; if these things worked for them, it's likely that they will work for you and your child, too.

- Give your child a diversion. Being idle can cause children to dwell upon their negative feelings and magnify their unpleasant circumstances. Distract them by giving them something engaging to do, such as embarking on a nature trip together, inviting their best buddies over to your house for games, enrolling them into a martial arts class, and so on. Keep their mind and body engaged to keep him healthy and happy – a deterrent to bullies who target psychologically weak individuals.

- Facilitate emotional expression. A bullied child will keep their feelings bottled inside. This is unhealthy because pent-up emotions can cause problems such as blood pressure abnormalities, asthma attacks, insomnia, and other health disorders. It also impairs the child's ability to handle stress well. Help the child in safely expressing these emotions. They can scribble out unspoken rants, paint a picture of innermost thoughts, or sweat frustrations out in a boxing gym. Doing so makes them release energy without hurting anyone. Keep in mind that it's not right to bully a bully; it only creates a cycle that hooks your child to aggression.

- Help children process their emotions. Feelings have thoughts attached to them; figure out if their thoughts are nourishing bad sentiments. Have a discussion about what's going on in their minds and what these notions are making them feel. Instruct them on the benefits of having accurate and empowering thoughts – having these makes people feel better and think more clearly. Make your kids realize that emotions are often temporary, and people naturally overestimate the length of time that an emotion will stay with them. Emphasize the importance of not acting out of transient feelings and encourage them to have something to hold on to (such as a belief, a positive memory, or a cause) when they're faced with difficulties and temptations.

- Help your child let go of the pain. It's not obvious at first, but some people can get addicted to pain and suffering because it provides stimulation, attention from others, and a sense of familiarity. Tell your children that they should not hold on to something that is harmful because it makes them miss out on better and more rewarding things. Let them see the beauty of life and the value of living a life free of unnecessary burdens. Although it may be hard because of the current situation, assure that things will change when they step away from a gloomy perspective.

- Be a good role model. Children learn from people who are important to them – give them what they need to cope not only with bullies but with other challenges of our daily existence. Embody the principles of building a strong emotional core and having healthy interactions with fellow human beings. This is among the toughest interventions especially if you were victimized yourself, but this may be the most significant action you can do. After all, you can't teach a child what you don't know, and you can't give what you don't have.

Raising offspring is a tremendous challenge but it gives the most rewarding experiences a parent could ever have in his or her lifetime. Think of the bullying incident as a wonderful opportunity to solder your relationship with your child and to build a strong foundation that will last long after you're gone. It will take long and hard work for you to accomplish this, but never give up. Persist and you will see your child grow both in body and spirit. And if you let love sustain your family in this dog-eat-dog world, you will unleash a life-empowering cycle that will go on from generation to generation.

Conclusion

Thank you again for purchasing this book! I hope this book was able to help you to fully understand bullying and to competently know what to do when it happens to your child.

The next step is to build your child's reliable arsenal against bullies and continuously work on developing his or her inner strength.

Finally, if you enjoyed this book, then I'd like to ask you for a favor, would you be kind enough to leave a review for this book on Amazon? It'd be greatly appreciated!

Thank you and good luck!

Printed in Great Britain
by Amazon

84867993R00031